ARCHANGELOLOGY

Raphael, Abundance Attraction Secrets, & Emerald Flame Healing Power (Archangelology Book Series 3)

ANGELA GRACE

Ascending Vibrations

CONTENTS

DOWNLOAD THE 11 + HOUR AUDIOBOOK 'ANGELIC MAGIC (ARCHANGELOLOGY 7 IN 1 COLLECTION)' FOR FREE!

If you love listening to audio books on-the-go, I have great news for you: You can download the audio book version of *'Angelic Magic: (Archangelology 7 in 1 Collection - 1. Zadkiel 2. Michael 3. Raphael 4. Metatron 5. Jophiel 6. Uriel 7. Spiritual Discernment)'* for **FREE** just by signing up for a **FREE** 30-day audible trial! See below for more details!

Audible trial benefits

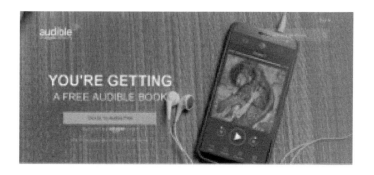

As an audible customer, you'll receive the below benefits with your 30-day free trial:

- A Free audible copy of this book
- After the trial, you will get 1 credit each month to use on any audiobook
- Your credits automatically roll over to the next month if you don't use them
- Choose from over 400,000 titles
- Listen anywhere with the audible app across multiple devices
- Make easy, no hassle exchanges of any audiobook you don't love
- Keep your audiobooks forever, even if you cancel your membership
- And much more.

Go to the links below to get started:
AUDIBLE US : bit.ly/angelicmagic
AUDIBLE UK : bit.ly/angelicmagicuk

GET YOUR *BONUS* VIOLET FLAME SPIRITUAL CLEANSING TOOLKIT

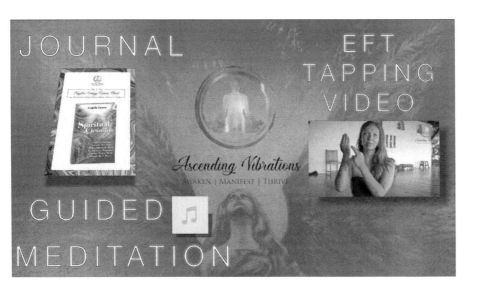

Are you ready to drop all the negative energy that no longer serves you?

- Easily use the violet flame to release blocks holding you back from greatness

- Cleanse your karma to skyrocket your joy
- Start growing spiritually again and get back on the path to your destiny

Violet Flame Spiritual Cleansing Toolkit Includes:

- 1. **Supercharged Energy Clearing EFT Tapping Video:** Download to Banish Negative Energy With the Archangels (Infused with 417 Hz Frequency)
- 2. **Spiritual Cleansing 7 Day Ritual Journal**: Daily Energy Cleansing Ritual Done-For-You; Simply Rinse & Repeat At Home (Print This Out, Stick It On Your Wall, & Cross Off The Days You Complete The Ritual)
- 3. **Powerful 10 Minute 'Spiritual Cleansing With the Archangels' Guided Meditation:** MP3 Download (Infused with 417 Hz Frequency)
- 4. ***BONUS*:** 10 Minute 'Violet Flame' Guided Meditation MP3 Download

Go to: *bit.ly/zadkielmeditation* **to Get Your *BONUS* Violet Flame Spiritual Cleansing Toolkit.**

INTRODUCTION

Have you ever felt lost? Truly lost? Many of us have felt this sense of being without a guide or purpose in our lives. I was certainly no different. Life can be brutal, and we often end up being hurt and wounded in ways that may not require a physical doctor, but these wounds threaten our existence nonetheless.

And so, we search. We consult healers and spiritual leaders, and we even try new and different concoctions from big pharma to try and feel better, when in reality, there are real and powerful guides out there who want to help you and to nurture you. Best of all, they can help you fill your life with abundance, healing, and courage. They can also give your life the direction to fulfillment. These guides are the Archangels.

From the many Archangels, there is a healing angel for every aspect of life. This book will introduce you to the healing, loving, and positively transformative powers of the Archangel Raphael.

While Archangels are divine beings, they possess an affinity for us humans, and they want to help us; all we need to do is ask them for assistance and guidance. Raphael is known for his kindness, healing powers, and guidance towards manifesting what you truly desire in your life. Your searching has brought you to this point, and your guide has arrived. Take

Raphael's hand, and walk the path of angels as you create the life you've always wanted but could never have before.

Here, you will learn about the history of the Archangels, especially about the history of Raphael. This will help you understand his willingness to help you, which is essential to your receiving the gifts he wants to share with you. Next, you will learn how to communicate with Raphael. Being able to call him in times of need, to thank him for his blessings, and to clearly ask for what you need is essential to forming a harmonious relationship with him. This is also not a once-off deal; you will be forming a lasting relationship with Raphael, and he will become an integral part of your life. Therefore, you can expect to enjoy bountiful blessings, healing, prosperity, and kindness to appear in unexpected ways throughout your life.

Perhaps the most powerful of Raphael's gifts is his ability to transform lives through a glorious cascade of hugely positive energy. You can tap into this energy channel through techniques such as using mantras or affirmations, as well as other energy manifesting techniques such as meditation, reiki, chakra and dream work, and the use of crystals. For the uninitiated, this may seem overwhelming at first. **It isn't.**

Fate has made you choose this book, and here you will learn all the essential skills you need to activate the power of Raphael in your life. This is a guided journey into understanding, selecting, using, and benefiting a life enriched with Raphael. From the techniques, approaches, and methods of countless people who have called upon Raphael, you will also learn to experience great peace, bounty, and synchronicity.

Part one tells you my story, and like I did, you will also find your way towards a meaningful and fruitful relationship with the Archangel Raphael, and while you may also create such bonds with other Archangels, it is likely that you will always cherish your bond with Raphael.

Part two is all about how to begin including Archangel Raphael in your life. This section is loaded with information, skills, techniques, tasks, and healing activities to help you manifest the powers of Raphael in your daily existence. Once you have gotten to know Raphael, you will carry his emerald flame throughout your life, spreading love and light wherever you go. Let me be your guide, and let's discover Raphael together.

ANGELA'S STORY

Welcome my brothers and sisters to the wonderful world of living with Archangels. You may already be familiar with some of the concepts involved in calling upon the angels for help or you may be a complete newbie—regardless, you are so very welcome to this space of learning, love, and light.

We all have a story, and like you, my story was not always the blessing it is now. I was searching for something more, even though I may not have known it at the time. Something was missing from my life, and I felt without a purpose as I struggled ahead. To those who didn't know me so well, I seemed to have everything working in my favor. I had a loving partner and a successful business. It seemed I was basking in wealth and adoration. What more could I possibly have wanted?

Some of you may find yourselves in similar situations to this. You have, like me, created a successful external illusion of perfection. When or if you ever mentioned not feeling complete, people may have looked at you like you were crazy. After all, what could you want when you already seemed to have everything?

However, as with all illusions, I had fooled others into believing a falsehood. I wasn't happy. I wasn't content, and I wasn't as blessed as I seemed. While I had some money, it wasn't enough for my lavish lifestyle, and I constantly worried about losing what I had. Even though I had savings, I didn't feel the real peace knowing abundance brought. You see, I had fixed my whole life around things instead of freeing my spirituality and embracing the awesome energies that surrounded me.

This journey into my spiritual nature would only start much later when I first encountered the powers of crystals and experienced first-hand their healing properties. I would love for you to read about this experience in *Crystals Made Easy*. My journey to angelology was a winding road, but I wasn't without guides on my inward journey. The angels were always there. Like a child learning to sit, stand, walk, and eventually run, I needed to learn how to tap into their powers, gifts, and guidance.

Have you ever had a moment of such pure and absolute otherworldly joy or tranquility that you thought you had imagined it? This was what my first experience with an Archangel was like. I had not intentionally summoned or communicated with him, but there I was, surrounded in complete and peaceful bliss. In the hectic world we live in, where we are told to harden ourselves and forge ahead, experiencing such a delicate and soft moment is not something we are programmed to process or understand. I certainly didn't fully comprehend what I had experienced.

The more I investigated the history and knowledge of Archangels, the more I began to understand how their presence in my life could channel energy and positivity to me. With these gifts, I could begin to manifest the changes I desired in my life. I could finally, and with intention, pray for the safety and health of those I loved. It was possible to even manifest healing and protection for my pets and for myself.

Best of all, I discovered the Archangels were not bound to a specific religious denomination. Believing in and connecting to the powerful Archangels didn't require me to change my faith or start subscribing to some alternative religion. I could start immediately. Using angelology in my life didn't require me to study for years or journey to some hidden temple. Everything I needed was within my reach, just like it is within your reach right now.

All I needed to begin was a little bit of knowledge and a small push in the right direction. Fortunately, my dear friend Linda had always been interested in and quite knowledgeable in all things esoteric, and when I one day raised the issue of angels with her, she immediately knew I had experienced a visitation. It was such a relief to know I hadn't gone mad, and there are actually millions of people worldwide who also interact with the Archangels on a daily basis.

Archangels do not always appear in the typical or stereotypical form we see in Catholic architecture. They may appear as light, invisible presences or as normal people.

Over several cups of herbal tea, Linda shared all she had learned about angelology, and I was instantly hooked. When I got home, I couldn't wait to begin my own research online or to contact the various internet-based communities who practice, discuss, and explain angelology.

One of the first things I discovered was that each person experiences their angelic encounters differently, and while those of us from a Catholic background may see our angels as typical angelic figures who stand there with a set of shining wings and a burning sword, many other people see them quite differently.

Whichever way you see the angels, they have the power and ability to enrich your life, bring you much-needed guidance, and facilitate fortuitous changes in your daily living. For those who, like me, have been searching for a way to make sense of life and a way to move forward with light and positivity, meeting, knowing, and embracing your angel guide is the beginning of a life-altering path.

Like me, you too can experience freedom from worry, courage to step forward boldly, wisdom to choose wisely, and the love to believe deeply in your life. Where I had spent my whole life believing I was nothing and wouldn't be happy (and therefore, I had to accept what I had and be grateful), I realized I had been controlled by people who didn't really know me and didn't have my best interests at heart. By finding the Archangels, I discovered who I really am, and I have since begun to create the life I deserved, which is so much more than I could ever have dreamed possible.

This revelation is also within your grasp when you begin the journey towards angelology. Now, it's time to learn all about Raphael and his amazing gifts.

INTRODUCTION TO ARCHANGEL RAPHAEL

Whether you believe in Archangels already or are still unconvinced, the truth is that they are real, and they are powerful. Being aware of them in your life is one way to enjoy the blessings of divinity in your life.

As with all the Archangels, Raphael's name has great significance. It means "God has healed" in Hebrew and gives us a strong indication of what powers Raphael has at his fingertips. He is a magnificent healer, and we can easily turn to him to help us heal from illness and recover from energy-draining experiences such as death and grief. Throughout history, Raphael has made several appearances in a great many diverse religions, making him easily accessible to people from all faiths.

RAPHAEL THROUGHOUT HISTORY

Raphael is one of the three most prominent Archangels, and many who believe and follow angelology summon him as well as the Archangels Michael and Gabriel. In the Bible, Raphael is the angel who stirs the waters of healing at the pool of Bethesda as mentioned in the book of John. This links him to the great healing you can receive from him. You can imagine the great compassion he must have felt to stir the waters regularly to enable healing and physical revival for those in need. Raphael also appears in Islam as the angel who blows the trumpet, announcing the resurrection and the last judgment. In the Torah, we learn that Raphael was commanded to heal Abraham from his circumcision, as well as to save Lot.

Throughout history, Raphael has been a force for good, and a powerful healer and facilitator to healing change. In the Book of Tobit, we also learn that Raphael had come to earth disguised as a man and journeyed with Tobit. During this journey, Raphael was known to have protected and healed Tobit. Raphael also bound up a demon who had been possessing Tobit's future daughter-in-law (See U in History/Mythology, 2019).

Lot was also saved by an angel who warned him to leave Sodom, and Raphael is the angel who forewarned him. This has caused many of the faithful believers to assert that Raphael is not only a healer but also a savior and a guide to lead us away from danger.

Sufism encourages the faithful to aspire to be like Raphael as he is kind, compassionate, caring, and brave. These are considered to be the best qualities, and even today, these characteristics are widely held as being virtuous. If you can begin to be like Raphael in the way you care for others, help those in need, and offer kindness and compassion to all, then you will begin to see him showing up in your life more often.

Raphael is, therefore, capable of delivering great healing and liberation to those who ask for his help and guidance. If we consider what he has done throughout history, then we can easily believe he can help heal illness, bind addictions to no longer torture us, as well as alleviate mental illness, and he can lead us to a life of abundance and freedom.

RAPHAEL'S HEALING POWERS

Throughout history, we find many stories of mysterious healings and divine guidance. While most will not feature a typical angelic presence, we may need to look closer at them as Raphael is somewhat of a chameleon when it comes to his physical manifestations. In the book of Tobit, he appeared as a man. He is often described as an unseen presence in the Bible, where he is said to have stirred the healing waters at the pool of Bethesda. Knowing

Raphael is close may be dependent on your perceptions and your spiritual awareness. However, his healing powers can't be doubted. Remember, he is the representation of God's healing on earth.

Being able to access his healing, request his assistance, and invite his presence is how you can begin to manifest healing and guidance in your life. Raphael is considered as the patron saint of travelers, healers, the sick, and the blind, and he is even attributed with the powers of matchmaking as he facilitated Sarah's first successfully consummate marriage by binding the demon who possessed her. Raphael is the manifestation of God's healing presence, and you can open the channels to that amazing healing and guidance in your life. So, how do you call on an Archangel?

When the waters at the pool of Bethesda was stirred, it was believed that an angel was near and the sick people who gathered at the waters would then be healed. It is believed that Raphael was the angel who would visit this pool and release God's healing on those gathered there.

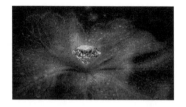

HOW TO EASILY CALL UPON ARCHANGEL RAPHAEL

Emerald green is often associated with growth and healing, and it is the color sacred to Raphael. Visualizing this color can help you quickly and easily connect with Raphael. Reaching out to Raphael is not a complicated process, and he is eager to help you. Like a dear friend who sees you suffering, he is only waiting for you to talk to him, to open up, and to let him in so he can help you heal.

Archangels have colors that are specific to each of them. For the Archangel Raphael, the color associated with him is a deep emerald green. While the Archangels are always around us, they do respond better when we are being specific in whom we are calling. Hence, when you start calling on an Archangel, it is a good idea to visualize the color of your chosen Archangel in the center of your forehead where your third-eye is situated. This is a powerful way to unleash your own energies and create a resonating call to summon Raphael into your life and into your mind.

HOW TO COMMUNICATE WITH RAPHAEL

You can instantly communicate with and connect to Raphael. When you are suffering a headache or the painful effects of an illness, all you need to do to reach out to him is to visualize yourself surrounded in an emerald green light. Some people prefer to see this light as a shower of emerald green sparks that settle on their body, melting into their being where these release Raphael's healing. You may even feel a tingling sensation in your body during this time. Whichever way you choose to see the light, you will be drawing from the Archangel's powers and, as you believe in his goodness and his willingness to help you, there will be an openness to healing in you.

This openness and belief in Raphael's powers are what will manifest the healing in your life. You can even imagine this like a friend who wants to help you. If you **believe** your friend can help you, and you **let** them help you, then they will quickly and effortlessly be **able to help** you. However, if you are constantly asking questions or doubting your friend's ability or their willingness, then you will delay and limit their ability to help you. To enjoy the full manifestation of Raphael's healing in your life, you need to accept and believe that he can and wants to help you.

Some believers choose to speak directly to the Archangel Raphael, and while there may not be a necessity for words, you can be assured that he will hear your call, and he will answer it. Raphael will not simply decide to help you on his own. He respects your right to choose, and he wants you to choose to call on his help. You may choose to call him by using some phrases such as these (below) to help you if you are unsure about how to speak to him in the beginning. What is most important is that you reach out (using whichever words you feel comfortable with); otherwise, Raphael will not be able to help you. You might say:

"Archangel Raphael, please help me."

"Holy Raphael, I call on you to be present in my life and to share your healing presence with me."

"Raphael, please manifest your blessings in my life today."

"Archangel Raphael, please answer my call and guide me through this painful time."

Archangel Raphael may also be called upon by using his sacred codes. Repeating certain numerical sequences channels the Archangels' energies. Calling Raphael may be done by repeating the following sequence, repeating each number 45 times: 157, 29, 125, 2129, 1577 (Purva Nimfa Magic, 2018).

REACHING OUT FOR BEGINNERS

Communicating with the Archangel Raphael is not exactly like hopping onto your phone and calling someone, though the connection may be even more instant than a phone call or message.

Connecting to the Archangel Raphael is about opening up, about receiving, and not just sending out a plea. So, like your mobile phone, if you are on airplane mode, you will not receive his guidance and healing if you are not switched on and fully present. It often comes down to whether you believe you are worthy of receiving his guidance and healing.

When you believe in your own worthiness and your ability to heal, you will be able to follow Raphael's guidance and increase your energy vibrations, which is how healing begins. Connecting to Raphael is about connecting to divine love. You are about to make the friend of a lifetime when you connect to the Archangel Raphael. Here are three ways to reach out and communicate with him:

- 1. Sitting quietly, imagine your body being showered by a bright emerald green light. Feel this light settle on your head, your brow, and your eyes, and feel it enter your crown chakra at the top of your head. As it soaks into your mind, you feel a wonderful and pleasantly warm sensation that slowly drifts downwards to rest over your heart. From here, you can feel this vibrant green energy pulse outwards to fill your body, raising your spirits and filling you with beautifully luminous emerald light. You can now speak to Raphael as he has felt your connection to his light and energy and has joined with you.
- 2. You may also choose to pray, invoking Archangel Raphael and the Almighty by whichever name you call on. Find a comfortable way to sit. You need not assume any specific prayer position, and you can even do this prayer while lying down. Now speak these (or similar) words of prayer: "Archangel Raphael, I call on you to join with my life, to become present in my life, and to share your higher energy with me on this day. I ask that you fill me with your healing energy and your bright light of love and caring

compassion. Let me feel the vibrations of your energy as it fills my body, gently reaching to the furthest corners of my physical, mental, and spiritual being. Today, I ask for your guidance and healing in the aspects of my life that have been weighing me down. Help me release the negative energies that have held me back from my divine destiny and limited the wholeness of my life." You can then continue to ask specifically for the things you want, such as healing from a physical illness, relief from mental strain or tension, and spiritual guidance. It's not important how you ask, as long as you ask.

- 3. When you have a conversation with someone, you may notice the communication has two phases: talking and listening. You have spoken to the Archangel Raphael, and now, you need to listen for his reply. While some people function at a higher level of spiritual awareness and may hear the words of the angels, there are other ways to listen for the Archangels' responses too. You could start seeing signs, feeling a heightening of energy or vibrations inside yourself, or feeling a presence near you (this would be a kind presence that is guiding you in the right course of action for your request).

You may think of the Archangel Raphael as a dear and wise friend; you have asked for his guidance and the gift of his healing. Now, you need to listen, watch, and receive that gift. Like with most gifts, you need to unwrap it. This means you need to accept the gift, decide whether you are going to place it somewhere so you can see and use it every day, or place it unopened in a drawer somewhere. Using the gift is up to you.

Communicating with the Archangel Raphael is not difficult. However, it requires your commitment to listen, to feel, and to receive the answers he offers you. If you are not open, you will not hear, feel, or experience him.

If you are still struggling to connect with Raphael, you may be bogged down in negativity, and until you find meaningful ways to lift yourself out of that lower energy, you will struggle to communicate and ask for guidance.

One of the biggest reasons why beginners struggle to connect with the powerful presence of the Archangel Raphael is that they doubt he is real and they doubt they have the right to even call on such a powerful healer and guide in the first place. These are negative energies, which will drain away your ability to listen and receive.

3

EXERCISES, MANTRAS, AND AFFIRMATIONS

Affirmations are positive statements that reinforce the great I am concept, which liberates you from negativity. Negative beliefs can hold us back and prevent us from connecting to the Archangels or receiving their gifts.

Many of us feel negative about our lives. Things happen to challenge us, and we often suffer bouts of depression and anxiety due to negative experiences. However, by embracing the positive energy of the Archangels, we can begin to transform our life view and our perceptions and build a wellspring of positive energy in our lives.

As with acquiring anything else in your life, it does not happen overnight, though you may wish you can just snap your fingers and magically be healed of all negativity. Instead, it is a journey where you discover the power of the Archangels, become more aware of them throughout your life and your daily existence, and learn to incorporate their positive blessings in your whole approach to living.

There are many exercises, mantras, and affirmations that will help you attract the positive blessings of Archangels such as Raphael into your life. We will look at some examples of this here:

TRANSFORMING NEGATIVITY

When you actively become aware of the kinds of energy in your life, you can begin to choose which energies you will channel or increase and which you will release and let go of. There are several energy transforming methods you can use, and they are all really easy to do. You don't need anything other than the powers of your mind and your intentions.

BREATHING EXERCISES

Sitting calmly, allow your body to settle, stilling the chaos within you as you focus on your physical existence. Turn your attention to your body. Note any tension or tightness in your limbs. This is a sign of negative energies having caused you tension and worry. Negative energy is destructive and it can poison your body and your life.

As you inhale deeply through your nose, focus on the sensation of your body lifting and growing tall like a bright green fir tree. Feel your seat, the soles of your feet, and even your buttocks being gently anchored to the earth. You are comfortably held in this relationship between the heavens and the earth.

When you are ready to breathe out, simply let the air flow out through your mouth, neither forcing it, nor concentrating on it. Simply note how the warm breath carries away all of the negative thoughts, memories, and emotions you have been experiencing.

Inhaling through your nose, allow yourself to feel a bright emerald green light accompany that breath. As it travels down your nose, your throat, and into your lungs, you can almost taste a green and verdant earth in the breath.

Repeat this process of inhaling life and positivity with each green breath and exhaling negativity and heated thoughts several times until you feel wonderfully at peace and ready to receive the blessings of Raphael. This is one of the ways in which you can open your mind and your heart to receive him.

From this point, you may want to move on to the transformative meditations where you will learn to practice cord cutting, clearing, and shielding.

TRANSFORMATIVE MEDITATIONS

Having calmed your mind and your body with the breathing technique just described, simply let your mind open like a vast lake that stretches for as far as the eye can see. Now form the name of the Archangel Raphael in your thoughts, bringing his name to your lips as you speak out, calling on him. You may choose to call on his guidance and his wisdom in healing you from a presence in your life that has proven negative and destructive.

"Archangel Raphael, holy angel who brings healing and transformation, I call on your presence in my life today. I call you to help me heal from a negative energy that has arrested my life. Help me to move past this blockage in my mind and in my soul. Archangel Raphael, guide me on a transformation journey as I cut the cords to this negative energy, this destructive person or event in my life."

As you speak these words, do so with conviction, even allowing some frustration to come into your voice if this is how you are feeling. Raphael is a healer, and he will never judge you for being upset; instead, he will only seek to help you and heal you.

"Raphael, clear me of this negative energy. Let the last shredded garments of this negative presence depart from my mind and my spirit as I look forward with power, positivity, and an energy that is made to serve all that is good."

In your mind's eye, you may begin to see the negative person or event that has been holding you back being enshrouded in bright emerald green light. You may even feel a strange sensation of being pulled as this presence fades away or tears from your life. Having a strong emotional response to this severing of the negative energies is quite normal. Do not be concerned by this; instead, enjoy the liberating presence of Raphael's light and love as he creates healing in you. Now you can ask him to clear away the last blockages this negative energy had created:

"Raphael, help me this day. I thank you for the negative energy you have removed from my life, and I now ask that you clear away the negative beliefs I have created as a result of this presence. The negative energy is now removed, blessings be upon you heavenly angel for healing me. Now, I ask your assistance and protection from the limiting beliefs I have built. Guide me to break down these barriers."

At this point, you may feel a wave of light wash over your mind and heart. You may even feel slightly lightheaded as your mind is swept clear of old beliefs that held you back. In this deeply meditative state, you realize you are worthy, you are loved, you are enough, and you are divine.

The powers of Raphael have channeled the holy presence of your maker into your life, and you are now free from any barriers or obstructions of belief that had previously limited you or held you back.

Now, you may ask Raphael for his protection and shielding presence to keep you from slipping back into negative habits and falling prey to negative outside influences in your life.

"Raphael, I thank you for helping, healing, and guiding me. My life is now filled with light, love, and potential. Lastly, I ask that you shield me with your awesome powers. Build a wall of light around me, casting out any who would seek to harm me or lead me astray. I am made stronger by your protection, and your guidance leads me down the paths I am meant to follow. Shield and protect me with your favor, your love, and your power."

You may form a mental image of yourself wrapped in a protective shroud of a bright emerald green color. Some meditators see this as a set of powerful arms that wrap around you in a comforting embrace. You are fully protected, and any negative thoughts or events simply slide off this protective shroud. You are safe and healed.

MANIFESTING ABUNDANCE AND HEALING

As from our discussion in chapter 2, it is important to believe what you are asking, praying, or wishing for. When your belief is strong, you can do anything. If you live with positive energy and believe you are able to do something, then you can and will do it. This belief creates the power to manifest what you need or desire in your life. While you may not necessarily open your eyes and be the owner of a brand-new BMW, you can attract and manifest the things you need and believe in within your life.

Once you have cut the cords to things that hold you back or push you down, you can clear the doubt and self-defeating behaviors you have been struggling with. You can manifest your own abundance and healing through the powers now at work in your life. There are several ways to engage in manifesting things you want:

AFFIRMATIONS

With Archangel Raphael having cut the cords that bound you, it is now possible to draw in positive energy and words of power to help you reach your goals. Affirmations are power statements. They are written in the first person as if you have already done what you wanted. Again, you need to read or say these affirmations to help guide you and to draw the potential into your life. When you speak with power and conviction, you will be ready to draw on and manifest your dreams.

Initially, you may struggle to come up with your own affirmations. These generic ones are suitable for your first meditation sessions. Once you feel more confident, you will be able to make your own specialized affirmations.

"I am free from negativity."

"Raphael has guided me to this truth: I am free."

"Healed and liberated, I walk into the light."

MANTRAS

Using a mantra during meditation is about creating a higher vibration to your energy. You influence the resonance or frequency of your spirit within your physical body. While affirmations are positive statements, mantras are power words you repeat at an increasing speed to help your body realign itself.

In Buddhist traditions, chanting "ohm" has the same effect, and it focuses the mind and brings clarity to your spirit or intention. While you reach periods of breathing in and out during your meditation, simply repeat these mantras, chanting them at increasing frequencies. You will feel an increasing building up of energy inside you, as if you are bursting to do something or say something. This indicates your vibrations have reached a higher plane, and you can now better receive the angels (Anglin, 2020).

Vibration increasing mantras include:

❖ Raphael's name
❖ Doing words such as "Heal" or "Lead" or "Guide"
❖ Angel words such as "Light" or "Love"

While there are many other techniques for communicating and experiencing the presence of the Archangels, these are some of the most powerful and easy to use. Through regular repetitions, you can build a foundation of knowledge and experience to help you regularly connect to and ask for the assistance of Archangel Raphael.

❦ 4 ❧

HEALING ANIMALS AND LOVED
ONES WITH RAPHAEL

Our pets hold a valuable position in our hearts, and they help us heal through their offering of unconditional love. Healing them and comforting them when they are ailing is something Archangel Raphael can assist you with.

While we have spoken in detail about healing ourselves, invoking the protection and healing of Raphael to help heal our bodies, minds, and spirits, as well as manifesting what we desire or need, we are also able to share that healing and protection with those we love. By drawing the healing power of Raphael into ourselves, we can channel that energy to those who need it. This is especially powerful when it comes to healing our pets.

Some people may believe it is strange to seek energy healing and angelic interventions for animals; however, animals were made by the same mighty Creator who made you. They are as entitled to healing, peace, and love as you are. You can ask for Raphael's assistance in soothing an ailing pet with a clear heart and mind. The Archangels love and care for all of the Creator's works, including people, pets, spirits, and angels.

While animals and people who are ailing can't always speak affirmations or utter mantras, they can receive love, light, and healing when you channel the angels' powers to them. In essence, you become a conduit, calling for healing and guidance on their behalf, and then relaying the energy and power as you receive it.

VISUALIZING HEALING AND PROTECTION

Sitting quietly next to the person or pet you want to help heal or protect, you can gently touch them, or if you are separated from them, you may also use a photo of them to help you focus. Breathe in deeply, letting the restful light of the Archangel Raphael enter into you with your breath. Feel all worries slip from your shoulders like a scarf carried off on the wind.

As you exhale, you are aware of being held by the earth, and as you inhale, you feel yourself reaching up to the heavens. Draw the positive energies from around you, feeling them settle on your crown, then penetrate down into your body, easing down your neck, spreading out over your shoulders, and finally, resting in your heart. Become aware of how open and inviting your heart is. This is where all your good intentions lie, and this is where you reach from to call on Archangel Raphael:

"Raphael, I call upon you. Come guide my hand and my heart as I ask for your healing on this dear friend of mine. Let your power move through me and reach into this kind soul who is in need of your healing and protection. I ask that you strip away the disease and illness that has brought them low. My request is that you fill me with your powerful presence and let this energy of healing and light and love move from my touch into this dear soul, bringing relief and recovery."

As you hold the pet or person you are healing, you can visualize a faint green glow starting to form along your skin. This is the light and love of Raphael, and it is moving from you to them, growing brighter and stronger as you continue to communicate to and receive help from Raphael.

Again, your belief is what will determine the level of transformation and transference of energy you can channel. You may use your imagination to help you visualize healing happening in their bodies, and from your touch, whether on their bodies or on an image of them, the green light spreads to envelop them in caring protection and divine care.

Focus on remaining calm and centered as you continue speaking to Raphael and calling on his help and guidance. If you feel anxious, you are allowing negative energies to filter in from outside, and this will not help the healing process. Instead, increase your frequency by adding in mantras or affirmations.

"Raphael, Raphael, Raphael, Raphael ... I call on you, Raphael. I plead your healing presence to be in attendance here as you heal this life. Heal. Heal. Heal. Heal. Heal. I plead for your healing and guidance. Let your light and love fill this being, this person, this animal with renewal of vitality and healing.

Let your power sever the ties of disease and illness which threatens this life. You have the power to release healing here and now.

This life is freed of illness.

This person, this animal is released from harm."

When you have completed your meditation, you may take a few moments to see the green light of Raphael's healing and love cover this life you hold dear. Feel the power of the Archangel move into them, protecting them from future ailment and a return of disease. You have shared the blessings of the Archangel Raphael with them, and you can believe they are healed and are now protected from harm.

ALIGN YOUR MONEY FREQUENCY WITH ARCHANGEL RAPHAEL

Wanting financial wealth and security is a human instinct, and in a world driven by consumerism, this is easy to understand. Raphael can guide you to all the wealth you need and deserve.

Many of us want to have a financially secure life. Fearing we will not have enough money, we often become worried and stressed, which can lead to health problems. While Archangel Raphael is known as the angel of healing, he is also known as the angel of abundance. This means he can lead you to abundant health, abundant life, abundant resources, abundant opportunities, and abundant money as a result.

As with other requests you may make of the Archangels, you need to invite the Archangels into your life. You need to let them know you are ready to receive their gifts and energies. This is a powerful example of the law of attraction at work.

If you are talking about something, you will align your life towards that thing which occupies your time and energy. This repetition is what increases your vibrational frequency, drawing the angelic presence of the Archangels near.

While you may not necessarily wake up one morning surrounded by bags of money, asking for abundant wealth may be delivered to you in a range of ways. It could be in the form of a new job that pays you a better salary. It could also be in the way of inspiration that leads you down a path to financial freedom. Asking to become rich is not a request that comes from a place of positivity or higher vibration. Being rich is rather associated with greed, which functions at a lower frequency. If that is your desire, you will struggle to connect to the Archangels as they serve higher purposes, not base desires.

Asking for abundance with an open heart is about leaving the solution open to the Archangels to interpret. Raphael may guide you to the means to achieve your financial goals (if they are about freedom and betterment and not greed), or he may bring resources into your life to help you achieve what you seek. Being open and receptive to the Archangel Raphael's responses is what will determine your successful abundance journey.

Your thoughts of money should be of such a nature that you see it as a positive aspect of your life, even when you have nothing. Dwelling on how poor you are will only attract more poverty to you. However, believing you have enough and knowing you will receive heaven's blessings as you need it will open the golden gates of abundance into your life.

Once you let go of fears of not having enough, your vibrational frequency changes, and you start calling on positive energies instead of bogging yourself down in negative beliefs. Believe you will be taken care of, and you will. Have faith in the abundance of your birthright as a human being, and you will experience all the blessings and abundance you require.

ATTRACTING ABUNDANCE

When you start changing the way you see money, you will begin the process of attracting abundance and wealth. Instead of looking at your bank balance and seeing zeros, you would rather look at all the things you do have, and imagine yourself having more of what you need. This does not mean you go on a shopping spree with your credit card and believe the Archangel Raphael will take care of the repayments. Instead, it is about opening yourself and believing you will be given all the opportunities and resources you need to make things happen in your life.

Abundance isn't a dollar sign. It is an alignment of factors, people, and places to help you achieve what you desire. Asking Archangel Raphael to bring abundance into your life may not result in you buying a winning

Lottery ticket, but it may be a chance meeting with someone who becomes interested in an idea you have and that landslide series of events that lead to you owning a Fortune 500 company or landing the job of your dreams.

Therefore, when you visualize the opportunities you need and the roads to abundance you require, you will attract the powerful transformative energies and the flow of Archangel Raphael's energy into your life. Whatever you need, you will receive.

Doing daily meditations and prayers where you call on the Archangel Raphael is one of the pivotal steps in achieving the life of your dreams. We will look at specific meditations in the next chapter.

❦ 6 ❦

ARCHANGEL RAPHAEL
MEDITATIONS

Meditations is another word for conversations. It is when you quiet your mind, your voice, and your attention, devoting it fully to the other person or being, and you listen to their responses to your requests. There is great power in meditation.

Meditating for specific goals where you seek the Archangel Raphael's guidance is within your reach now. In this chapter, you will be able to follow specific meditation scripts to help you reach your goals and achieve a greater connection to Raphael and receive his blessings.

ABUNDANCE ATTRACTION WITH ARCHANGEL RAPHAEL

Sit comfortably, close your eyes, and breathe in deeply for five seconds. Hold for a moment, and then exhale slowly, letting the air pass over your lips for five seconds. Again, pause for a moment before inhaling for five seconds and then exhaling for five seconds. Do three more repetitions of this breathing in and out.

Once you have completed the pattern, simply breathe normally, letting your eyes rest comfortably as you let them close and open softly. Do not focus on anything in particular that may distract you. Instead, you turn your focus inward to the area over your heart (your heart chakra) and feel a warm presence there.

Rest your hands on your thighs or in your lap, making sure to relax them into an open and receiving position. Inhale as you begin to visualize a bright emerald green shower of light descending upon you. The light lingers on your body, clinging like glitter to your hair, skin, and limbs. You can feel an angelic presence, shrouding you in light, love, and abundant spiritual wealth.

Visualize what it is that you want. If you want to ask for something specific, you may. If you want to ask for abundance in general, you can also do so. Perhaps you want to ask for an opportunity or Raphael's blessings and presence for an important meeting today. Allow your mind to relax, slowly melting the tensions in your body as you open yourself to the abundance flowing from heaven and from Raphael into your life.

You receive this precious gift with an open heart, thanking Raphael for his guidance, care, love, and light. Allow yourself to experience an increased energy and vibration as if you know that which you asked for is about to happen.

"Archangel Raphael, I thank you for your presence today. Thank you for your care and love, your compassion and abundant guidance as I step towards my destiny under the protection of your wings."

Throughout your day, be mindful of the signs of Raphael's presence as he guides you towards achieving the abundance you asked for. You may see a neon green sign above a shop you frequently visit or you may be struck by the emerald green tie your new boss is wearing. These are all there to let you know you are on track.

MEDITATION FOR HEALING WITH ARCHANGEL RAPHAEL

Lying comfortably in your bed, close your eyes and allow your body to sink into the covers, softening and sinking ever deeper and deeper. Become aware of the earth below you and the heavens above you. Inhale deeply through your nose, letting the scents of the earth bless you and fill you. Draw the precious oxygen into your lungs, and when you exhale, imagine the breath you have just breathed being carried upwards to the heavens.

You notice a small firefly sparking above your head, gently flying lower and lower, and eventually it lands on your hand. The small body is flashing a brilliantly green emerald light. Soon, it is joined by other emerald green fireflies, and they all land on your body in a dazzling shower of light.

The fireflies have a soft vibration in their bodies, which they share with you. This energy fills you, sinking into every pore of your body and filling you with great calm and peace. You are aware of an angelic presence near you, and you say his name: Raphael. The bright emerald green light now covers, protects, and nurtures all of your body, mind, and spirit.

Can you feel the presence of Raphael next to, around, and inside you? Like a child, safely carried in the arms of their father, you are safely wrapped in the wings of Raphael. The pleasant warmth of his nearness soon travels through your body, and you can feel it gently vibrate whenever it encounters an ailment. If you have a headache, you feel the warmth fill your head, easing tension and pain. If you have a mental concern, you are made aware of his healing presence even there, soothing your troubled thoughts and bringing you peace and clarity. Healing is happening as you lie wrapped in his presence and peace.

Closing your eyes, you thank Archangel Raphael for his care, compassion, and healing. A warm tingling sensation in your body fills you and acknowledges the healing Raphael has shared with you this day. Breathing normally, you may find yourself drawn into a deep and peaceful sleep. Simply relax, knowing Raphael is watching over you, guarding and guiding you.

MEDITATION FOR LOVING YOUR BODY

This is a wonderful meditation to do in the bath or shower. Place your hands and arms in a warm self-hugging position. Feel the sensation of your skin touching skin. Close your eyes and let the water of the shower or bath cover your skin, tracing down the curves of your body and warming your physical existence.

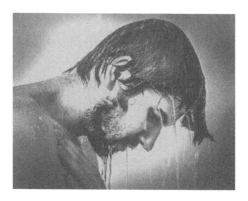

Let the water run off your body in green waves of soothing, nurturing, and loving light.

Inhale deeply, feeling your ribs move, pushing outward against your self-hug. Exhale and feel the same sensation of being held on the outside of your arms now. The Archangel Raphael is holding you, protecting you, easing your worries and concerns, and connecting to your body. Breathing normally, allow yourself to luxuriate in this deeply nourishing and loving exchange as his energy moves through your skin in waves of green light.

Speaking aloud or in your heart, thank Raphael for his presence, for his nurturing of your body, and for his love of your physical presence. Express your own love of your body, telling yourself you have a beautiful and shining soul. Your body is the home of your spirit here on earth, and it is a temple. Archangel Raphael has shown you the virtue of your wonderfully alive existence, and you can feel inner peace overflowing in your mind. Thank Raphael for coming to visit you and promise to love your body from this day forward, treating it with dignity, respect, and compassion.

MEDITATION FOR LIFE DIRECTION

Entering a meditative state, close your eyes and breathe in deeply, exhaling fully before inhaling again. Let the peace and radiance of the Archangel Raphael enter and sustain you. Feel an emerald green light glowing inside your mind, calming, soothing, and easing any mental tension and worries you may have.

Feel your mind expand as you allow the guidance and wisdom of the

Archangel Raphael to fill your mind. Welcome his presence in your mind, your body, your spirit, and in your life.

Speak to him in the volumes of your spirit and mind as you ask him to guide you, to direct your path, and to lead you to the destiny you have been seeking. You may ask him to take your hand and to show you where your life is going, to help you understand the path before you.

Remember to listen to the responses and replies Raphael has for you. This is a conversation, and he will answer you in the most unexpected ways. Be open to receive his wisdom and guidance. Remember to thank him for any guidance he gives you, even if it's not what you had imagined or hoped for. Simply open yourself to accept that the Archangel knows your destiny, and while it may not be fully revealed in one meditation, you can always return to this safe and spiritual space and communicate with Raphael again, gaining further insight as your life direction is revealed to you.

ARCHANGEL RAPHAEL
MANIFESTATION, CHAKRAS,
DREAMS, CRYSTALS, AND KARMA

The chakras are energy centers in the body. By releasing any blockages or channeling energy through different sections, you can open your body and spirit to receive energy and become a conduit to the powers of heaven. From your root chakra to your crown chakra, you are a connection between heaven and earth.

There are many supporting theories and methods to communicate with the Archangel Raphael, and these can help you to better connect to him, receive his blessings, and understand his guidance. During your meditations, being aware of your chakras will help you process the presence of divine energy in your body, as well as opening your perceptions by using your third eye or mind chakra to see and understand the messages and presence of Raphael.

When you are not fully open to receiving the wisdom and guidance of the Archangel Raphael, you may find that he approaches you in your dreams, which may require some analysis and interpretation. However, he will always find a way to connect to you when you have called on him. Sometimes, that calling need not be vocalized or even conscious. There have been many people who felt his presence and experienced his blessings in dream form as their subconscious or spirit called out to him.

Crystals are truly remarkable elements that can help you connect to the angels, and since they have healing properties too, they offer you a double benefit. Using crystals can help heighten your vibrational energy, opening you to the higher guidance of the Archangels. Malachite and emerald are the crystals most strongly associated with Archangel Raphael. Both are a wonderful green with malachite having darker swirls of green in it, and they are known to promote healing and can revitalize your body. Holding a malachite or emerald crystal in your hands while meditating will heighten your experience and draw the Archangel Raphael to you. Crystals, essential oils, and irises are a great way to strengthen your call (Acone, 2010).

Crystals come in a range of colors, and their unique qualities allow for the refraction of light waves at different points on the electromagnetic spectrum. This light is energy and vibration. Holding an emerald means you are holding the vibrational energy of that part of the spectrum. This is also the frequency Raphael moves in.

MANIFESTING ABUNDANCE

To fully experience abundance in our lives, we may call on Archangel Raphael to help us heal from previous traumas, and using crystals can help facilitate this process. Emerald is known to align with our heart chakra and promote physical healing. Malachite also aligns with our heart chakra, promoting spiritual healing (Hibiscus Moon, 2017).

Placing the crystal on your body, where you feel a need for healing or on your third eye chakra can help channel the energy and vibrational presence of Raphael there. Using crystals helps you to increase and focus your energy for manifestation. The stronger your belief, the more powerful the results.

MANIFESTING COURAGE

Having courage in today's world is about being strong enough to persevere in the face of trials and challenges. In the Bible, we are told by God to take courage "for he has overcome the world," and this indicates how we too should manifest courage in our lives. Asking Archangel Raphael to help you manifest courage is one way to do just this.

The solar plexus chakra is associated with courage, and by placing an emerald or malachite here while you meditate and call on Raphael, you will channel the powerful energies and guidance he delivers to the place where your strength comes from.

In your dreams, you may see an emerald green and golden light emanating from this area of your body, indicating Raphael is busy creating courage in you, releasing doubt, and healing your strength center.

MANIFESTING WEALTH

None of us want to be poor. We cling to what we have, desperately seeking more. However, Archangel Raphael told Tobit that "Those who give alms will enjoy a full life," meaning that when we give, we receive. This is the law of karma and the law of attraction in action. Generosity of spirit will lead to a manifestation of wealth in all aspects of your life. This could be spiritual, physical, and financial wealth.

Talking to Raphael, you may find yourself asking for money, but this limits what he can do for you. Instead, ask for an openness and a manifestation of wealth. Remember, Raphael is the power of God's healing on earth, and he can perform miracles and wonders you can't even begin to comprehend. When you meditate on this and allow your hands and your heart to open, you encourage a flowing of energy and good things will come to you. Wealth untold will manifest in your life.

MANIFESTING POSITIVE CHANGE

Many of us use the term karma quite loosely to mean we believe what we put out, we get back. If we do good to someone, we believe good will be done to us. Likewise, if we undercut someone, we can expect retribution to occur. To correct our karma, we need to engage in positive change. Raphael can help you with this. His healing presence can help you ease tensions not only in yourself but also in the relationships around you. By asking him to help you heal a particularly troublesome relationship, you can draw his healing and supportive energy to that aspect of your life.

While you meditate about the person or relationship you are concerned about, you can call upon Raphael to guide you to finding a peaceful resolution to the conflict. You can replay the situation or past events in your mind, letting a glorious wave of emerald green light wash over the memory, coloring the people, places, events, and words of that memory. Soon, any negative associations you have with that person or event will be washed away and fade into the background of your mind. You may find the next time you meet that person, they behave differently, and you will also act with a different energy towards them as Raphael guides you in peace.

Calling on the Archangel Raphael to manifest wealth, healing, and guidance in your life may seem like an illusion to the newbie. You may think it's just your imagination when you see green light or feel his presence. However, imagination is the freeing of your mind, and only when you open your imagination can you begin to communicate with the Archangel Raphael. Use your imagination; don't hold back.

You may see the crystals that you use glowing or casting brilliant green light on your body, and you may wonder if you are imagining their vibrations or heat. Do not let doubt drain the energies from these moments; instead, go with it. Use all the skills you can to manifest the presence and gifts of the Archangel Raphael.

❧ 8 ❧

HOW TO TELL WHEN
ARCHANGEL RAPHAEL IS
AROUND

Seeing incredible green light is a sure sign Raphael is nearby and working his awesome powers for your healing, compassion, and protection.

While Raphael appeared as a man in the book of Tobit, he does not need to physically appear to guide and influence us. There are a range of signs to help us experience the loving compassion of Raphael. When we see these signals, we can be assured Archangel Raphael is close and his gifts are flowing through your life.

THE SIGNS

The signs range from thoughts, feelings, colors, images, and experiences to words that suddenly enter your mind. Look for these signals in your day as you pass through life (Virtue, 2010):

Sparkles of Emerald Green Light

People have reported seeing a bright light of emerald green color, announcing the presence of Raphael. This light can be in your mind as a vision or it can be sudden signs or places that have this light quality.

You may be sitting in a verdant garden, or you may be traveling to a place where you find yourself in green surroundings. Raphael is letting you know he is present.

Messages

Raphael may leave you messages in anything from the headlines of newspapers to license plates. Be alert to messages from him telling you he is near, he has healed you, or he is helping you. Once you see this message, don't forget to thank him for his intervention and intent towards you.

His Name

When we need a little reassurance, Raphael is quick to step in and let us know he is near and he has his guiding and protective wings over us. Many people have reported seeing his name or words of comfort when they needed a sign most. This can be in signs, names of places, and even in newspapers again.

Appear In Your Mind

Many people who have been ill reported seeing Raphael in their minds, and while doctors would write this up as delirium, these people can clearly describe seeing Raphael. The presence of him in our minds is not a product of an overactive imagination—he is real. Seeing him in your mind can be incredibly soothing, and people speak of his larger than real presence, which fills them with healing and peace.

Tingling and Vibrations

Many of us have suddenly experienced a vibration or tingling sensation before when we call upon Archangel Raphael. We may also feel a sudden sense of warmth as if someone is hugging us. Others report feeling the hair rise on the back of their necks as they sense his power. It could also be a sign of his healing in your body as his energy penetrates into your cells, organs, and limbs.

Suddenly Finding Resources

Raphael wants us to learn and to heal, and while he is eager to give us his energy, he also wants us to use it in our lives. He will often guide us towards the healing we need. This may be suddenly finding the doctor you needed or discovering a book on spiritual healing that resonates with you. Either way, Raphael is guiding us towards healing.

Singing and Music

All of heaven is singing. We are quite familiar with the concept that the angels sing, so it isn't much of a stretch to believe that the angels will also communicate with us through music and songs. When you need a special message, Raphael may suddenly speak through a song on the radio, or you will discover an album that soothes you in your time of need. Even birdsong can bring you an easing of tension and lessening of your physical and emotional burdens.

Image 16: The sound of singing, music, and the lyrics of songs can be the way in which Raphael communicates with you. Be alert to the messages of these cheering you up, showing you compassion, and helping you heal.

A Gut Feeling

Many people have done miraculous things simply acting on their gut feeling. They have saved people and avoided disaster, and they have found prosperity in just listening to their instincts. When they think back on these events, they might even say that something told them to run, to invest, to go for a meeting, to make that appointment, or to change their habits. This "something" is Raphael. He whispers hints and suggestions into our ear, and this leads us where we are meant to be. He will never force us to choose something, and we need to really listen to that inner voice to fully benefit from his guidance. We have free will, and we need to choose what will work for us.

WRITING A LETTER TO RAPHAEL

Letter writing has traditionally been how we communicate with friends, reach out to them, get to know them, and share with them. Raphael is your friend, and you should show him the same care and friendship as you would a dear friend who helps you without any thought of return. Writing a letter is one way to do just this.

YOUR CLOSE FRIEND

S tart by writing a letter by hand to Raphael. Take care in selecting beautiful paper, and perhaps use a special pen for this. You are showing your attachment to and love for your dear friend, Raphael. In your letter, share your hopes, wishes, desires, and dreams with him. Express your gratitude for what he has already done for you.

This letter is a great way to communicate with him about those you wish to heal or help. You might write something like:

> *"Dear Raphael, thank you for being my friend and guide. I value the healing and prosperity you have brought into my life. Today, I wanted to tell you about my dear friend Lisa who is struggling to make ends meet. She is a kind and dear soul, and I wish her health and abundance. Could you please work the energies of abundance*

in her life and could you help me to assist her? Thank you for your presence and support. Love, Rachel."

This letter need not be miles long, and it need not be filled with academic language or poetry. Simply write to your friend, Raphael. Talk to him, tell him about your wishes, share with him your challenges. When you open up your communication to him, he will also maintain a more constant presence in your life.

Lighting candles is about bringing light and love into your life and the space where you meditate. The elemental flames light more than just the candle; it also lights up your spirit.

READ YOUR LETTER

Let your letter sit in a special place in your home for a day or two, then have a candle ceremony where you read the letter aloud to Raphael. You may choose to combine this with a meditation or mindfulness session, perhaps having your emerald or malachite crystals near, burning some incense, or lighting aromatherapy candles.

Read your letter aloud, letting it become a conversation between you and your dear friend, Raphael. Speak it like a plea, telling him more about your desires and wishes. There is no need to be formal, though you should be respectful. Remember to listen and wait for his responses. Over the next several days and weeks be aware of signs of his presence in your life as he begins to answer your requests and guides you towards the abundance and healing you asked for.

You may also receive visions or dreams in which you see the solutions or healing you requested. Write these down as soon as you have them. Later, you can reread these, and if there is anything that is unclear, you can always meditate and communicate with Raphael. He is patient and kind, and he will always clarify what he meant and guide you to a better understanding of his energy and how this will manifest in your life.

Importantly, when you receive feedback from Raphael, thank him for his attendance to your needs and wishes. A grateful heart is an open heart, and this is what you need to receive the guidance of the angels.

❧ 10 ❧

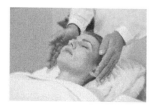

ARCHANGEL RAPHAEL REIKI

*Reiki is about transmitting energy, encouraging energy flow, and dissolving blockages
that affect your health, your chakras, and your spiritual well-being.*

R eiki is energy healing where the practitioner channels energy by raising their palms. The presence of crystals can amplify this technique and channel the energies towards specific body parts where ailment exists. Light or energy workers use this method to communicate with and channel the healing powers of the Archangel Raphael to those in need. While this method may be quite foreign to you, you can use it successfully when you communicate with Raphael and receive or transmit his energies. Whether you want to heal yourself, a loved one, or a pet, this method is very adaptable and effective.

ARCHANGEL RAPHAEL REIKI MEDITATION

Sitting comfortably, allow your body to soften and gently find the most natural position for you. Breathe in the vibrant energy of the Archangel Raphael and breathe out the negative energies of a day of toil. Feel the bright emerald green light of Raphael enter your body, bringing energy and transformation to every cell of your being.

Raise your palms, facing them towards the person or beloved pet you want to help and heal. In your mind, you may call on the assistance of Raphael; however, it is important to be still, to allow yourself to empty as you open, and to allow the healing energies of Raphael to pass through you and into the subject of your healing.

Be mindful of the living world around you. Draw those powers and verdant energy into you, letting it flow through your palms like the mouth of a river to cascade down on the one you love.

Let your mind be still as you channel the love, healing, and inner bliss you feel to those who need it. You are now a still point that shares positive energy and compassion with those who are in need. Let them drink the energy, divine mercy, and guiding presence of the Archangel Raphael from your hands.

Like watering a garden, you shower down blessings to the pet or loved one you care about. Allow your energy to move outwards like ripples on a clear pool of water. You are part of an ever-expanding wave of energy that heals and protects those around you.

If you become distracted, simply focus on the surface of your palms. Let the tingling energy and vibrational frequencies settle on your body, move into your cells, and circulate through you. Then allow the channels to open from your palms, sharing the divine blessings of Archangel Raphael with others.

HOW TO SPEND TIME WITH
ARCHANGEL RAPHAEL

Having Raphael in your life is a constant stream of positive and healing energy. He becomes an integral part of your life and habits. Having him near allows you to channel divine energy on a daily basis, and we need never feel as if we are asking too much or receiving more than our share. As long as we are grateful and express our gratitude, as well as share our energy with the world around us, we are more than welcome to take Raphael's hand.

Archangel Raphael is known to be a compassionate healer. This means he knows our weaknesses and our flaws, but he loves us nonetheless. Since he is such a wonderful friend and powerful presence, many of us choose to make him a part of our daily life. He is not simply a presence we turn to when we have nowhere else to turn. Instead, his guidance can and should become a daily exchange of energy and wisdom.

DAILY LIFE WHILE CARRYING THE EMERALD FLAME EVERYWHERE

Archangel Raphael is not only there for the big stuff. He wants to help you with all aspects of your life, from the tiny headache you have to the doubts that you have before going on a date. If you let him, he will even guide you to your soulmate, like he did for Sara and Tolbit's son.

You can speak to him on a daily basis, and he will never tell you "go away, I'm busy." Instead, he wants to help you, and he is all around you, waiting to share his guidance, love, and compassion. How wonderful is that!

Some believers carry an emerald or malachite pendant around their necks to remind them of Raphael's nearness, and they keep a constant channel open to him. Experiencing real health, well-being, and compassion for others is not something you only dream of. It is something you live daily by including Raphael as part of your everyday life. Thanking him constantly and carrying his emerald flame of light everywhere with you will make you a lightworker who shares their blessings, love, and compassion with those around you.

With the daily guidance of Raphael, you can transform your life and lead others to this awesome friendship and wellspring of healing energy. Raphael wants to share, and by showing your gratitude to him and sharing his gifts, you will become a blessing to others.

AFTERWORD

The road stretches before you, but you no longer walk it alone. You never did. Now, you simply know this irrefutable truth. The creator has sent his Archangels to hold you, keep you safe, heal you, guide you, and befriend you. Archangel Raphael is here, now, and he is at your side through this life. It is within your power to connect to him, to call on him for guidance, healing, and counseling when you are struggling and even for the small steps you take through life every day.

Having learned how to call Archangel Raphael and how to meditate on his guidance, presence, and caring, you can now boldly reach out to him whenever you need him. His presence in your life will continue to help you be a more grateful, energetic, and spontaneous being filled with light and love that will attract abundance, friendship, and love to you.

I encourage you to share your journey and the protection of Raphael with those in your life, to make his presence felt, and to continue to develop as a worker of light, whether you practice this as a career or simply as your contribution to the human race.

Lastly, I would like to leave you with this prayer:

May light and love travel with you on this day,
I pray for the protection of Archangel Raphael to guide you

to carry you on his wings and to bring you solace
for any hurts you may have suffered.
I ask that he lead you to the abundance your life deserves
and that he holds your hand in friendship
and in love as he holds mine with his other hand.
I pray for light and I pray for peace to comfort you
in darkness and in doubt
as I reach out to you my brother, to you my sister.

REFERENCES

Acone, S. (2010). *Crystals to Help Connect With Archangel Raphael*. Healing Crystals. https://www.healingcrystals.com/Crystals_to_Help_Connect_with-_Archangel_Raphael_Articles_1791.html

Anglin, E. (2020). *How to Raise Your Vibrational Frequency: Channeling the Angels*. Learn Religions. https://www.learnreligions.com/raise-vibrational-frequency-1729268

Hibiscus Moon. (2017, February 22). *Crystals for Working With Archangel Raphael* [Video]. YouTube. https://www.youtube.com/watch?v=7aOAuOkj-7c

Meditatia. (n.d.). *Guided Meditation Reiki*. Meditatia. https://www.meditatia.com/guided-meditation-reiki.html

Peroshini. (n.d.). *Archangel Raphael. About The Angels*. http://peroshini.-com/peroshini/About_The_Angels.html

Purva Nimfa Magic. (2018, September 22). *Raphael-Archangel Raphael-157,29,125,2129,1577* [Video]. YouTube. https://www.youtube.com/watch?v=kPi-HXGj7XVQ&list=PLCMPRCPVXHGcmAYIIO2MjkDs_Dc4EECkb&in-dex=4&t=0s

See U in History/Mythology. (2019, October 21). *Archangel Raphael: The Angel of Powerful Healing - Angels and Demons* [Video]. YouTube. https://www.y-outube.com/watch?v=7kdipeG-IZU

Virtue, D. (2010). *8 Signs from Archangel Raphael*. Beliefnet. https://www.-

beliefnet.com/inspiration/angels/2010/06/healing-miracles-of-archangel-raphael.aspx

Virtue, D. (2016). *Archangel Raphael 101. You Can Heal Your Life.* https://www.healyourlife.com/archangel-raphael-101

ILLUSTRATIONS REFERENCES

Image 1: ptra from Pixabay https://pixabay.com/photos/angel-castel-sant-angelo-rome-wing-2677047/

Image 2: Dimitris Vetsikas from Pixabay https://pixabay.com/photos/archon-michael-angel-archangel-2086750/

Image 3: Mark Hultgren from Pixabay https://pixabay.com/illustrations/portal-gateway-pool-door-exit-454462/

Image 4: Thomas Wolter from Pixabay https://pixabay.com/photos/green-leaf-gem-emerald-plant-4928714/

Image 5: Jan Vašek from Pixabay https://pixabay.com/photos/iphone-template-mockup-mock-up-500291/

Image 6: Lirinya from Pixabay https://pixabay.com/photos/watts-mud-dirty-foot-feet-1012402/

Image 7: Gerd Altmann from Pixabay. https://pixabay.com/illustrations/brain-think-thoughts-psychology-4065092/

Image 8: John Hain from Pixabay. https://pixabay.com/illustrations/woman-power-glory-affirmation-2128020/

Image 9: No-longer-here from Pixabay. https://pixabay.com/illustrations/dog-paw-hand-love-friendship-2383071/

Image 10: S K from Pixabay. https://pixabay.com/photos/money-dollars-success-business-1428594/

Image 11: Okan Caliskan from Pixabay. https://pixabay.com/illustrations/meditation-spiritual-yoga-1384758/

Image 12: Olya Adamovich from Pixabay. https://pixabay.com/photos/man-male-model-person-young-979980/

Image 13: Aloysius from Pixabay. https://pixabay.com/photos/gems-stones-crystal-gemstone-836763/

Image 14: LillyCantabile from Pixabay. https://pixabay.com/illustrations/reiki-alternative-yoga-healing-4133336/

Image 15: My pictures are CC0. When doing composings: from Pixabay. https://pixabay.com/photos/meadow-bokeh-nature-dew-dewdrop-4485609/

Image 16: Dieter_G from Pixabay. https://pixabay.com/photos/birds-swifts-singing-twitter-music-2672101/

Image 17: stempow from Pixabay. https://pixabay.com/photos/hands-writting-invitation-typography-2110452/

Image 18: Pexels from Pixabay. https://pixabay.com/photos/ash-candle-light-candle-christmas-2179184/

Image 19: Jürgen Rübig from Pixabay. https://pixabay.com/photos/wellness-massage-reiki-285590/

Image 20: Aaron Cabrera from Pixabay. https://pixabay.com/photos/worship-singing-inspiration-church-4088561/

YOUR FEEDBACK IS VALUED

From the bottom of my heart, thank you for reading my book. I truly hope that it helps you on your spiritual journey and to live a more empowered and happy life. If it does help you, then I'd like to ask you for a favor. Would you be kind enough to **leave an honest review for this book on Amazon?** It'd be greatly appreciated and will likely impact the lives of other spiritual seekers across the globe, giving them hope and power.

Thank you and good luck,

Angela Grace

Why not join our Facebook community and discuss your spiritual path with like-minded seekers?

We would love to hear from you!

Go here to join the 'Ascending Vibrations' community: bit.ly/ascendingvibrations

Printed in Great Britain
by Amazon

84767455R00038